Doubt & Circuitry

Poems

by
T.D. Walker

Doubt & Circuitry

Poems

by T.D. Walker

Southern
Arizona
Press

Southern Arizona Press
Sierra Vista, Arizona

Doubt & Circuitry

By T.D. Walker

First Edition

Author: T.D. Walker
Editor: Paul Gilliland
Formatting: Southern Arizona Press
All Artwork: Pixabay.com and CreateVista.com

Published by Southern Arizona Press
Sierra Vista, Arizona 85635
www.SouthernArizonaPress.com

ISBN: 978-1-960038-32-6

Poetry

Dedication

For DK, wise voice

Foreword

I started on the poems in this book in 2020 as a way to explore the turns in my own thoughts about the pandemic, particularly how the information I'd received from various media was both alarming and, oddly, consoling. Although I heard again and again on the radio about death from COVID, I also listened actively for ways I could protect us at home and in the larger community. So, we stayed in. We masked. We homeschooled the children. We did dozens of other things to keep safe.

The pandemic kept my children at home for a good fraction of their young lives, and my husband and I did all we could to shield them from its direct effects. But we couldn't keep them from a sense of isolation.

Then, we saw the world opening again after vaccination made that possible in 2021.

"Chernobyl 1986 / COVID 2021" began as a question: how did the disasters of the 2020s shape my children's view of the world, particularly in light of their disconnect from the world? And my own? How would they begin to function within the world again?

As a long-time radio enthusiast, I'd read about Duga, also called the Russian Woodpecker, which might have been part of a Soviet radar system constructed to spy on the west. For years, its chirp could be heard on radios that could receive the frequency at which it transmitted. I'd also read about the possibility that Chernobyl had been built to power the radio transmitter. Not long after the meltdown disaster in 1986, Duga went silent.

This disaster disconnecting metaphorical mother from child made me think more about how I was coping with parenting while being so disconnected from the world during the pandemic and after it was, ostensibly, over. Obviously, the magnitude of the pandemic was far less than that of a nuclear reactor meltdown. We sheltered at a home we weren't driven from. But I wanted to examine more closely how communications--external, including from the government, as well as internal, in my family and in my own head--went dangerously awry during both.

I'd finished the final poem of the book, "Chernobyl 1986 / COVID 2021" at the end of 2021, the year of hope in the form of a vaccine.

Then, in February 2022, crisis struck again near Chernobyl, when Russia invaded Ukraine. The subject of the poem became the subject of tragedy once more. After spending a while grappling with the ethics of writing about something that was a presence in my childhood, but at a far distance, I added the coda.

I conclude that "a poem is never the way things end," which is a belief I've long held. Poems open the world, give us pause so that we may question what we think we know. Writing these poems has certainly given me cause to question what I thought I'd known about the pandemic, conspiracy theories, and wars imagined and brutally real. Poems lead into what's possible, and thus I hope these poems serve as a reminder of the power of asking questions that require deeper and more sustained attention.

Much gratitude to those whose time, energy, and wisdom fostered this book:

to Shannon Connor Winward, for her critiques of individual poems in the book;

to Shannon and to Joshua Gage for their comments on the manuscript as a whole;

to Joshua and to Laura Cox for their thoughts on my notes to accompany "Fierce fighting" for *The Cities and Memory Project*;

to Paul Gilliland for accepting and crafting manuscript into book, and to the journal editors who believed in the merit of the individual poems in the collection;

to Stuart Fowkes for including a poet in a sound project, and to Thomas Witherspoon for posting the call for participants on his website, The SWLing Post;

to Valerie Reiss and to Wendy Van Camp for our monthly accountability check-ins and all our talk of progress on manuscripts and gardens;

and most of all, to Justin Fisher and to our children, our sweet signals in the noise of the world, for showing me what beauty is possible even in the smallness of isolation,

thank you.

Contents

Chernobyl 1986 / COVID 2021

CONELRAD 1960 / COVID 2020

I. Invitation

1.

What should I say I remember
about our isolation? Shudder-
signal, silence? Your script
cycling the invitations you wrote?

You sent us loping, nearly summer-
feral, dog following, casting our neighbors
flag-emblazoned cards: Drinks, fire-
works, the metal hull of a grill --

What should I say I remembered?
You held my list, snapped in a clipboard,
pen tethered through the hole in the clip.

You asked if we were shopping for a spring tea,
toilet paper balanced against your knees.
I lifted you from the cart so more would fit --

2.

You lifted fruit from the mold so more would fit:
olives cross-sectioned, anatomies of shrimp.
Lime-based and mayonnaise-strange capsule
gelling into place. How it all cooled,

hummed into being by refrigeration. Space,
you thought, was a little like that, the way
rocketmen train for enclosure. They don't want
us, below, to see how little room they can inhabit --

I shifted the paper towels, the antiseptic
bottles in our cart half-bashed and suspect
but all we could find. The brilliant burnt-red

marigolds, impatiens, cosmos frilled and pink:
from what was left of the low seed stock,
we'd shape our waiting from what we could get --

3.

You shaped your waiting into a halter
-dress, a Liberty print that summer
I'd craved the way I wanted the boys'
slack-grounded wandering through July.

You'd warned me away from their cache,
whispered the ways explosions damage
bodies, buildings. You warned us
disaster happens all at once --

You shaped your waiting into canals
dug through the backyard, worlds
Martianed and cut by the child-sized steel

tools we'd bought you: the garden
rake's bent teeth, the hoe's corrosion,
the shovel's splintered wooden handle --

4.

The ladle's tarnished silver handle
bathed in vinegar. Hibiscus petals
adrift on the punch surface: superheated
entries or reentries? Rocketed

captains might know, or a dog (Soviet).
I pick up your small radio, tune it,
holding my breath as I pass those two
small triangles, Phobos, Deimos.

What I began to realize I couldn't handle
arced around us but refused to settle.
April-thrilled, I asked you if you thought

binary stars each believed the other
orbited it. You flung another shovel-
load of wet red clay agglomerate --

5.

The load of wet red ground
meat you shaped and seasoned --
(let's pretend your father did this,
you whispered over the radio's hiss) --

He explained it to me once, CONtrol
of ELectronic RADiation. If bombs fell,
we'd hear the pattern of silence, voice, silence.
(My mother shouted, "Go greet our guests.")

The load of wet red ground proved
unsuitable for the cosmos. What grew
contained the distances between children

and neighboring children. Can we play,
the boy next door asked. ("Can we," not "can they") --
I broke you from them, returned you to the garden.

6.

I broke from the guests, returned through the garden,
clutching the dog. I thought I'd broken
the radio. After I'd turned the wheel,
short silence broken by falsetto wail,

broken by silence. Instructions, Phobos,
Deimos, those twins of airless war, demigods
shouting fire over fireworks. Seek
shelter, the voice instructed. Under attack --

We broke from the world. You trenched
shelter in our backyard, turned over our bomb-drenched
concept of waiting out disaster --

Did I hear tornado sirens? EAS tones shrieking?
Instead, you huddled together over a bud, calling,
"Mom, come here, come over, look closer" --

II. Alert

1.

What should I say I heard,
isolated with a thousand Hertz
tone? The announcer apologized --
interruptions are necessary. Phased

voice from transmitters miles apart
reading the text of the local alert:
suburban north Houston or the entire Gulf Coast,
my room or the mesh of Independence Day guests --

What should I say you heard?
Jump-screened, the online class you hid
yourself from? Kindergarten flickered,

aura-obscured, buffered, delayed
the way my voice skips during migraine,
skips as if the illusion of a trapped bird --

2.

(Skip, Father explained, like a child
bouncing off the ionosphere, made
signals reach us that weren't ours --
like doubt, we make ours what we hear.)

"Nuclear bombs," the man said. You
wound the camera after the group
photographs: fire, fireworks. Film
exposed to radiation becomes its signal --

We skipped class together. I withdrew
you from the experiment of online school.
In shielding you from more exposure

to screens (or mere exposure's effect?)
am I teaching you what you should neglect?
When we hide, even families become more nuclear --

3.

When I emerged, bearing the nuclear
threat on my radio, I couldn't hear
you calling over the guests for me --
"Not the Soviets, not the Chinese,"

(as if naming each threat lifted it
from possibility) -- his voice, static,
mine shouting for you, reverting
("Mommy!"), his again, "No earthling --"

Patterns emerge. I change the wording,
teach you not to <u>love</u> the flag. "Pledging
allegiance to the [fill in the blank]

shows how we love our country, one
nation, [indivisible as a cell's wall]."
I want to teach you to question the book --

4.

You questioned the alert. A dance orchestra
interrupted by a Martian invasion, a drama
you'd heard before. How you loved *his* voice, news
bulletin read on Halloween years

before I was born. The announcer's false
calm not the despair of the dramatist's.
Once upon a time, there was a planet (Mars),
whose creatures succumbed to a virus --

You questioned the book's perforations, crude
diagrams of plants, answer keys, the concept of school
(home or otherwise). You hid beneath

paintings of storm-dead trees (each season
a lesson in what can die) drought-blighted, diseased,
yard-bound and frozen, a sketch of a "vaccine" --

5.

Yard bound, I held the radio's hiss.
No shelter. From the Communists,
silence or the fear of the signal. Flags
pinned the neighborhood together, grass

selvages edging the unsewable fall-
out shelter. As if you'd told the soil,
(belted against what flows, breaks, surfaces,
red (clay) shifts), this is what you cannot cross --

Unbound, you split the day, forced its nucleus
outside. Cataloged the jays, the dark-eyed juncos
we'd fed maize and the sunflower seeds you'd found,

head-bound and browning. Everything becomes screen-
like, if not actually a screen. Glass, a hard freeze,
the idea of an electron, what we are able to ground --

6.

Doubt: an electron run to ground. The guests
mingled, a few laughed at the nuclear bomb "test
alert" I held. Static (another explosion) background
figures arranged themselves against -- sound

exploding from the street -- fireworks, hands,
hands grabbing me from the uniform grass --
children's (some my blood) hands, a game
(static, crash) played to learn what will come --

You played a structure into place. What will come
bound to crisis is either parasite *or* symbiote,
(possibly both). You want to talk photosynthesis,

solar energy, solar eclipses. Windmills and stillness.
How the Moon pulls away from Earth, inches
each year like a child repelled (or repulsed?) to independence --

III. Shelter

1.

What should I say we meant by *shelter*? Children
shelled and camouflaged, trenched, hidden-
insect tense, unmothered nestling-drab, grub-deep --
we pushed into the woods, past suburban creep,

jay-calling our way toward silence the space
hissing between radio signals couldn't place.
Our numbers young and vague, first-hatched
larvae of spring, fretting the creek's dun edge --

What should I say you meant by shelter*? Our home*
stinking of us, as if we'd collected dung and bones
(our own?) over a year? We pushed out cracked shells,

tendons, entrails of time we'd consumed. Time,
we'd thought, clung to us, parasite-sure, fulsome --
time strung with a lack of what should be possible --

2.

Time struck us with a lack of what should be possible:
Space breached, but not this red clay soil.
How you once told me the way wind levers
trunks of exposed trees, how storms sever

roots from from tap roots. We'd make fallout
shelters from what had fallen. Hollow
trunks, (toolless and toothless as we were)
hollow our bodies for what we thought was nuclear --

Time-struck, I fell into what had once been possible,
("There's nothing like the taste of Blue Bell -")
white-ridged watermelon rinds, hammocked magnolias,

not the ghost-edge of ice cream you summered through
bending spoons (your father said buy a scoop):
detail will always prove something meaningless --

3.

Details proved meaningless to us. Tetrahedron:
faces pine-branched (family *Pinaceae*). Sun
quivering against the evening's carapace --
sky rocket, bottle rocket -- you found us,

huddled in our dry-needle nest. Tetrahedron:
your halter dress against your collar-bone.
(After, we never pinned our patterns, aligned
ship lights, Roman candles obscured by pines --

Details slipped from us. ("Things are changing
at --.") Hanging the curtains I'd made, I sang
your names into the past ("There's more

for your life at – "), imagined us (as I pulled
shades) packed tight against the unmasked crowd,
firecracker tight ("- is your savings store") --

4.

Firecracker tight, we made shelter: you hid
within us. How difficult it is to judge
distance, to judge how massive the craft
listing over the city (what must have

been the city) must have been. How fast
we'd made our shelter, then, trespassed,
(a fuse lit) we became shelter. We did not
need to judge the velocity of what has stopped --

Firecrackers, tight against the evening. Fourth
day of a month you mark in bites. Welts soar
dry treetop high: flitted sparks against sodium lights

wake us. I try to remember summer-thrilled
caps, sparklers, Roman candles others held --
how I clutched my ears, how I clamped my eyes --

5.

How I clutched my ears, how I clamped my eyes --
(What good judging the crowd's speed and size?
One ship, one spark thrown from a neighbor's
match -- what good judging the pine shelter's

switch from walls to bonfire frame?) You fled
(what good judging) what the bodice of yard
held flat: a small fire in the grill you doused,
a dud firecracker your sandaled sole squelched out --

How you clutched your sense of the world, snagged
evidence of now, of a possibility of now from my past --
how the ice cream truck passed, playing "The Music

Box Dancer," how the nowness of you heard
children (not you) baffling against the curb --
how you asked me to explain, again, red shift --

6.

How, you asked me to explain, red shifting
guests from burning to the possibility of burning --
the space our shelter made pushed outward, bodies
accelerating apart from crises or safety from crises:

Smoke-gauze over the crinoline edge of the ship.
Later, you told me how you thought the taffeta-crisp
fracture of what had been in the woods behind the house
was you, unable to move soundlessly in a vast white dress --

How you asked me to explain what we'd read. Shift
countries around your mental map like seeds left
unpacketed until too late. You explain the lines

I write, not letters but hungry animals, unplaneted.
Dirt means nothing more than dirt. Red clay, packed
root-binding tight becomes an absence between rake tines --

IV. Aftermath

What should I say *happened?* It could have
had implications, the way fire or lack of fire can save
neighborhoods. Houses were built where pines
burned. Or trees fervor rooted to reclaim

land. No more houses were needed
than we already had. The attack seeded
military investment. Or we surrendered. The world
seam-ripped from itself. Or what you gathered --

What should I say happened? It could.
"After," we've yet to check off on the curriculum.
We talk about what we'll do after the virus

has gone as if the virus could read the prim-handed
workbook clocks stopped each on the hour. What happened
closes us, a chapter, a cell wall. That must, for now, for us,

be enough --

Doubt & Circuitry

Are There Any Long-term Effects of Ionospheric Heating?

"A good analogy to this process is dropping a stone in a fast-moving stream. The ripples caused by the stone are quickly lost in the rapidly moving water and are completely undetectable a little farther downstream." -- from the University of Alaska Fairbanks HAARP FAQ [1]

-- or, instead, say the sea, say baroque rock dropped astern.
Say consider the hull of a cruise ship, consider the tension

water maintains as its surface. And then consider
breaching that surface, consider falling through water,

consider movements of fins in water, fins in vocal folds.
And consider the algae, the fish, the whales among the shoals,

stone-wavelets' undulations faint against receptive skins.
Consider the eyes, convergently evolved therein --

Say the sea. Say baroque. Say what can be seen,
received. Say tentacles of giant squid, say manatees,

say giant oarfish, say giant Pacific octopus. Consider
failure to capture the wholeness of a being. Say sea-quaffed limb,

say how the stone falls toward the sediment-edged dim-
ness of things. Consider how I too am made monster --

Fierce fighting in substantial numbers: ships damaged,

ships sunk. Artillery, air defense weapons, and other heavy

equipment. Ships, aircraft and missiles, helicopters, aircraft;
tanks and artillery, aircraft and a helicopter, tanks and artillery.

Ships (a secure bridgehead, firmly established, a secure
base, landings not opposed). Warships (sunk) a Sea

Harrier (missing), aircraft (shot down), helicopters
(destroyed on the ground). Missiles and guns replying --

Troops. Commandos. Regiment. Casualties. Some
prisoners taken. Troops. Garrison. Troops. Men

Twenty-one are feared dead. The loss of many young
lives. Troops ferried in, without their equipment --

The meeting was adjourned until later today:
Public emergency sessions. Mass for peace arranged --

*Lines in this poem are from a 1982 BBC World Service shortwave radio
news bulletin covering fighting in The Falkland Islands.*

Can HAARP Be Used To Generate VLF or ELF, that is Very Low Frequency or Extremely Low Frequency Signals?

"However, the HAARP facility does not directly transmit signals in the VLF/ELF frequency range. Instead, VLF/ELF signals are generated in the ionosphere at an altitude of around 100 km (more than 62 miles). Frequencies ranging from below 1 Hz to about 20 kHz can be generated through this ionospheric interaction process." -- from the University of Alaska Fairbanks HAARP FAQ [1]

"The youngest stude upon a stane, /   The eldest came and pushed her in." -- from the folk song, *The Twa Sisters* [2]

Consider, too, how I was made monster.
Once (again), you say: drowned woman. A river

arced her body, crest and trough, until the miller plied
her sinuous: sternum-violined, distal phalanges aligned

pin precise. No mermaid, no story of a mermaid's
siren voice. Not that. Never that. Let's call it a whale's, then.
    flayed

open to reveal what bodies always reveal. What the fiddle sings
harrowing through some low signal sent to submarines --

If I too am playing to a court, consider
which among you is my beloved, which my sister.

Consider who (you think) threw me in and who rends
strings that were never veins. If my voice's low ghosts

shudder meaning into the resonance of your bones,
consider what it is to be an instrument --

When you asked, I was a diagram,

                                        promising
movement. Unbuilt, a time machine,

doubt and circuitry. Is this the point where I begin? Regret,
like time travel, resists the corpus of the present.

I've seen transmitters fall. I've held the coiled
wires that might have made lucid

signals through which I could have known. You
asked, and I was unable to say anything then but *no* --

Strange diagram I was then, unable to say *yes*,
lag of unfit parts, currents

flowing the wrong direction. I rewrote myself,
holding each *no* I'd said until it flipped, shell-

cased the machines of desires lost and switched.
Designed (too late) the woman we'd wanted to exist --

Can *HAARP* Control or Manipulate the Weather?

"No. Radio waves in the frequency ranges that HAARP transmits are not absorbed in either the troposphere or the stratosphere —the two levels of the atmosphere that produce Earth's weather. Since there is no interaction, there is no way to control the weather." -- from the University of Alaska Fairbanks HAARP FAQ [1]

Consider, too, what it is: to be an instrument. *Seeding* a peculiar
word for that dance of silver iodide through clouds, though
    dance

demands a body. Tanks heavy with the idea of snow, planes
pluming chance over Idaho[3]. Snow or its lack watched, from
    Doppler

radars wheeled to where that snow might fall. Or not. Consider,
    too,
hurricanes bombed. Your word, *bombed,* though weather
    control in war-

time is banned. Why stop at weather? You changed the climate.
    Made storms
more powerful in warmed oceans. Or maybe not the *particular*
    you,

sunning yourself in theory. Let's look at the sun. Let's look at
    what layer
solar radiation snags green above tundra. Let's look at what you
    assign color,

red, firing meaning into ionosphere. Meaning, yours. Let's look
    at theory,
yours, too, what hangs high enough to be mistaken for
    complexity. Control,

when it happens, when it can happen, holds close, branching
    like snow
falling through clouds, branching like signals just beyond your
    hearing --

Transcript

Were you showing me the pattern of my name
exploded, coalescing into equations you wrote?
Calculus, but for Liberal Arts majors,
as if you were teaching us some different

elegance in elegant things. I don't remember
derivatives now, or how to find the rate of change.
Memory isn't continuous, leaves its chair,
does not adhere to rules of chains --

How could you have shown me the pattern of my name?
Triangular lights in the dusk you didn't arrange --
Some clue that would help me track my difference.

I'm still sitting outside some austere brick building,
untaught, particular, watching the sky for flickers in the evening.
I still believe in UFOs, in memory, in coincidence --

Can HAARP Create an Artificial Aurora?

"The energy generated at HAARP is so much weaker than these naturally occurring processes that it is incapable of producing the type of optical display observed during an aurora. However, weak and repeatable optical emissions have been formed using HAARP (and reported in scientific literature) and observed using very sensitive cameras." -- from the University of Alaska Fairbanks **HAARP FAQ** [1]

Fallen through clouds of high-energy particles, what pricks
    needle-
urgent somewhere in the castle you've made against my signal?

Stone weighing on guarded stone. I'm not reducing myself to
    tales
collected in dark forests. Or elevating myself. You ask if
    molecules

excited by my signal can make an *artificial aurora.* In the
    original,
remember, her name was Briar Rose, Talia, Rosamund. Source
    material

tells us that, left unguarded, left sleeping, she (what was her
    name?) had twins.
Aurora was the daughter to which her mother couldn't consent --

You've told me your story. Mine is weak against the sky, though
    I can tell it again,
repeatable, the way experiments yield expected results. The way
    rumors bend

light into patterns you want to see. What it is to be an instrument
sensitive enough to pick up my signal, unaided. What it is to
    want

sleep, so that someone might come into your father's house and
    slant
light onto your face. How disastrous the kiss. How
    immeasurable the princess --

confession as simulation #1

you disappeared as you spoke. another professor
hunched into oak. sparrows fled my ribs. my daughter

(unborn unspeaking) hallowing campus wrens. students, low-
voiced (they knew whose identities I'd stolen). my own

disturbance stolen, and I am cast carillon on the bench, a queen
fretting her own return. cross streets. will they send the bus. the
    trees

said prayers for you all. I (thought I'd) begged for a cat,
begged for my place in the auditorium's alcove. an anchorite

witnessing the miracle of someone else's father
turning into my father. I drew: ash line, chalk line. my finger

turning over the pill in my palm. the only way I could stay
seated in class for long. at least I had the excuse of migraine.

at least I had the excuse of trying to tell *them, then.* Say, open
    your mouth,
anchorite, and go. say, faithless, faithless. say, remember what
    faith

                                        (and go) --

Can HAARP Exert Mind Control Over People?

"No. Neuroscience is a complex field of study carried out by medical professionals, not scientists and researchers at HAARP." -- from the University of Alaska Fairbanks HAARP FAQ [1]

Light on a hypothetical face, the electrode's kiss: How
    immeasurable
thought becomes measurable, spinning like a magnet.
    Everything spins

patterns to you. Spider webs in trees, or your memory of them.
    Wires too thin
to be mine enter the specific region of the brain, stimulate the
    responsible

structures to activate or deactivate them. This is not how I want
    to say it:
angle of a surgeon's hand threading probe past arachnoid layer.

Electrical pulses finer than the last dissent of an ensilked moth's
    wing. Or
pulses aimed through the placed wire where the pathological
    episodes sit --

Look at me. Not the way I've been captured in stone or oil, a
    saint
staring out from a sacred wall, holding arrows at my ribs or head,

waiting for the moment the story makes sense of my patient
suffering. Look at me. Not at the way you memorized sand-

stone creations. Look at the patterns I make in the ionosphere,
no more the story of a sea monster than a rock dropped astern --

Chernobyl 1986 / COVID 2021

Note: In 1986, Chernobyl's Reactor 4 was destroyed during a test that went horribly wrong. The surrounding area was evacuated and much of the forest around the nuclear reactor site was cleared away. To contain the radioactive materials leaking from the site, a metal "sarcophagus" was built over the reactor, though some material escaped containment. Later, the New Safe Confinement building sealed the reactor and sarcophagus more completely. There is some speculation that the Soviet Union built Chernobyl to power Duga, a massive over-the-horizon military radar system, near Chernobyl. This poem takes that idea as its starting point.

I. Witness: Or, Duga Recounts the Meltdown of Chernobyl's Reactor Four

1.

You expect me to give you history: mothers
returning to land once deemed too radio-
active, tongues of Geiger counters
clicking away as I once did. Launch echoes,

missiles I'd been trained on. I'd heard
shuttles instead, astronauts. Spark-winged
birds I'd been nicknamed for. Swerved
flights leaving Earth, braced for their returning --

You expected me to give you history, your mother
born the same year as the Voyagers
crowned their way toward interstellar space,

born the same year as the first Chernobyl
reactor began tearing apart worlds:
broken-cored, hard-skulled as a shelled virus --

2.

Broken cord: hard-skulled as I was,
pecking echoes from dead-branched
diplomacy, how could I hear her voice,
suddenly cut? The sand-drenched

attempts at controlling her came later.
Witness, memory: havoc releasing neutrons,
nuclear forces breaking my connection to her.
I remember her feeding me, then we were broken --

Broken chord, unskilled as I was,
teaching you meant remembering music
I'd abandoned with my body years ago.

You expected me to give you letters,
numbers, a sense of freedom from crisis:
Listen, I taught you which fears to follow --

3.

Listen: she taught me which fears to follow.
When they test you, they test connection.
Chasing the arc of Space Shuttles. Echo
movement of my radar, seeking locations

upward, forward, of what might have met us.
She taught me when we were together
repetition gives us freedom. Silence
again and again meeting my receiver --

Listen, I taught you which fears to follow
your questions with. What work to show
signaling what you understood of addition,

addition's opposite. What did I teach you?
You waved your small hands in our picture window
while I pulled toward the moment of vaccination --

4.

While I pulsed toward the moment of reaction
separating us, what signals did I lose?
A deer paused, perhaps. A fairy-tale maiden
touched her neck. Did she hear a bird's voice

warning her of the specifics of desire? I envied
patience with which she waited for the birds'
movement against the trees, as if some *envoi*
escaped their wings. Then, I felt the surge --

While I pulled toward the moment of vaccination,
(Fair Park, gates echoing the Ferris wheel within --
we all want to be held and moved), signs

instructed us to listen to a low-powered FM
station. How we were promised one thing and given
another shot. How shielded and vulnerable in these lines --

5.

Another shock: how shielded and vulnerable in these lines,
connection between us, or so I thought. Had I seen her,
solid against the forest around us? I'd seen her sacrifice,
containment of what could kill us all. One doll inside another:

concrete, zirconium, uranium, electron shells, then at the
        nucleus,
particles clinging together like frightened children. Scattered,
children become an army. I'd seen her sacrifice. A village
built for her, children fissile in the trees, for her, reactor --

Another shock: how "shielded" and "invulnerable" in these lines
we were given after, how we were meant to return to lives
we'd led before as if you, too, had been given a chance at safety.

Schools opened, parks, playgrounds. The State Fair
beckoned families. Our masks marked us cowards.
If only you were still contained within my body, my immunity --

6.

If only I were still contained within her: power
tested, taken from her. Do I still see the moment
fire and stone overtake the night sky? Her tower
blown, do I still see smoke against firmament?

And still, her other reactors kept us screaming
pulses into the darkness. You tell me this was only one
tower she'd lost, one of four. Still producing
heat, the promise of heat into the April dawn --

If only you were still contained within my body, my immunity
towering against the unmasked, the denial of what keeps rising --
smoke billows up as quickly as numbers, mutations.

Instead, I take you inside my work. They deny
rising numbers, mutations, the uncontrolled virus;
how can I deny you the shelter of my remaking --

II. Sarcophagus: Or, Duga Considers the Concrete Shelter over Chernobyl's Reactor Four

1.

You expect shelter, when you're a child
disconnected from the shelter you'd known:
Look, they poured sand over her, melted
uranium, what they used to control

reactions in uranium together into a *lava*. Did they
consider what it is to be volcanic? Let's be precise
here, now. I'm scientific, an instrument, an array
reaching out and back. Lava proves Earth's breached crust --

You expect shelter, when you're a child
sheltered for almost a third of your life.
I tried to rebuild our world. Globes and maps

gave us a sense of where we were and were
just once. You wanted to go back to the art
museum. That carefully pieced-together past --

2.

Mausoleum, that carefully pieced-together past
covering you: not a sarcophagus, but a womb
unable to keep you in. A mausoleum, vast
chamber holding many bodies, like a test, like a hand --

But they called it a sarcophagus, a coffin, as if
only one body were contained within. Mine
kept its chirp and beat, still listening for death
pressing toward us through the clearing sky --

*Museums we carefully pieced together, passed
our time in or the illusion of our time. Even masked
we were never safe enough to feel our breath*

*pausing in front of the real. We retreated to the screen.
We were patient, or you were, waiting for vaccines
awaiting approval, like waiting for ourselves --*

3.

Abating her fuel, like waiting for myself:
I watched the fire rage for nine days, for some
paradise lost. I watched the liquidators, the forest
they brought down around us, radiation

beating against the trunks like a mad beak.
I watched them haul away once children-
laden branches, watched them clean streets.
Watched as they surveyed ways to seal her in --

Evading school, like uprooting yourselves,
you pace this house become show-and-tell
(nothing of the external world remains

long at our fist of a door before we quarantine
boxes, envelopes, bags. How long viruses cling,
how long we keep our hands from our faces --

4.

How long I kept my hands over my face
until they built hands over her, joints
unsealed, letting in the rain, the ice --
hands grasping some raspy-voiced

prayer. Sarcophagus, inadequate church,
scaffolds telling the stories of murdered saints.
You'll tell me to make of the smoke-stack's reach
steeples releasing connection's remains --

How long I kept your hands from your faces,
each surface in the outside world a virus-
laden threat. I took you to on walks, crowded

trees keeping us from contact with others, urged
you to touch nothing. You asked me how the air curled
particles we couldn't see into movement we could --

5.

Particles I couldn't see burned into movement they could
measure: what escaped from her sarcophagus fissures.
How much she must have loved breaking worlds:
she broke the firmament they built over her.

First, the pines came back. Did I want to break her
tomb, release her, reconnect with her? Or with that place
recovering from her half-death? First pine, then birch.
Bears, wolves. Then birds, but they avoid old nests --

*Parts you couldn't see became movement I'd yet
make: had I forgotten the deep collective breath
musicians take before beginning a song?*

*I was vaccinated, I had to make my body
unlearn its fear of movement, had to carry
you or if not you then the world back home --*

6.

You, or if not you, then the world broke the home
sheltering what was left of her. How long had I been
disconnected then. How long until they began a new dome.
Three years after her disaster, I fell silent.

Was it because she could no longer carry me?
I'm not sure I noticed when they stopped my song.
I watched in silence as they covered her, steel
arc the largest thing ever moved on rails. But I said nothing --

You, or if not you, then the world: your home
cracked open. I watch you running in the park nearly alone,
just ahead of us. I can't ask if what you see,

wind-like, is the connection between us breaking
your idea of what it is to be family.
What it is to be home, the only place you've been --

III. Half-Life: Or, Duga Watches the Grandmothers Return to the Exclusion Zone Near Chernobyl

1.

You expect me to tell you about the grandmothers. Instead
I'll ask how many ways there are to destroy the earth, or
this piece of earth I cannot leave. The only place I've been
able to hear her. I've compared atoms to Earth before,

become tedious with listening for news of her. Other worlds
break, magma becomes lava, what we see as giants'
surfaces can panic into storms. Even radiation isn't ours
alone. Enough of that too can destroy us, even from a distance --

You ask me to tell you about my grandmothers. Instead
I tell you about yours. Tell you about how they made
homes your father and I came from, how they bound

family and our ideas of family. None of this is mine
alone. Instead, we drove for days, counting turbines
turning over the flat land between home and home --

2.

Turning through the forest land between home and home,
they came. At first, I thought of them as transmissions,
signals sent to target then returned, as if their echoes
shuddered back anything about where they'd been.

Echoes of an elsewhereness that would absorb
who they were. So they came singing their return
here in the small houses they'd known. Birds
avoid old nests. Women knew what would burn --

Turning through the walls of your grandmother's
home, paintings of flowers. Hadn't I taught you before:
annuals die, leaving their seeds behind?

Each grandmother leads back to another
question: where. As if she could be here,
as if death were a movement in place, in time --

3.

As if death were a movement in place, in time,
they returned from the gray, governable towers,
returned to their tools, attempted to tame
overgrown gardens back into something wilder --

Decay is like that, slow, a kind of progress. I heard
their tools scratching the earth again. My transmitter
disconnected, what else could I know but the ground
turned up to accept what was offered?

As if death were a movement in time, in place,
like force, like seasons, all the rudimentary science
I'd offered you. Sound dies, the weakening signal,

echolocation. Light dies at opaque surfaces, planets
die, stars consuming them in their own deaths.
Plants die, animals die. Viruses too, we say. People --

4.

Plants die, animals die. Vitrify too, we say. People,
given a few hours to collect belongings, had paused
mirror-like in front of them: first, the reactor explodes,
then everyone must seal themselves in a new future. Lost

all but a few pictures. Everything belonging to children
forced to stay. Children or our ideas of children bear resilience.
But that was years ago. When the grandmothers returned,
did they take the paths their children ran through the forest?

Plants die, animals die. Viruses too, we say. People
remain as images, obituaries, regrets. This cell
we've created, bee-like, distinct, readable as a golden disc:

shelter as stories of ancestors born between plagues.
I recite names, places. I recite dates, mark the space
unanswerable now, shaped by questions I might have asked --

5.

Unanswerable now, shaped by questions she might have asked,
does she watch the women returning home? How can she
tell me, now that she has been tested, taken apart, masked
again, what it is for her to see them, grandmothers singing

land back to itself. She wasn't a bird, burned from within.
Still, her body lies, feet grasping some uncaught prey,
or grasping some predator escaping her unfeathered skin.
Watch them with me, praying over her bones, then walking
    away--

Unanswerable now, shaped by questions you might have asked,
these years shrunk by a virus we might have contained. Not lost.
You question the size of things, wonder if we are made of
    smaller

parts, smaller ones within those: when do we end?
I try to explain atoms, nuclei, electrons, spaces defined
by our inability to grasp them. Is there love in our failure --

6.

My inability to reach them -- is there love in my failure?
What else can I do but resonate their footsteps on this shared
    land?
You don't believe I can hear their movements, the way they
    fracture
earth. This is theirs, isn't it? Cesium's half-life already passed --

True, I can't tell you what they say to each other
besides *return*. Does it matter that I cannot
speak? I want to lie down near them, dog at their fire,
listening. I want to lie down near them, silenced, spent --

Your ability to reframe home: is there love in this failure
to leave? I've given you images of playmates here, peers
you chat with online in half-hour blocks. You want to run

green lengths near the creek with them, fuse
your idea of who they are with the thrill of presence --
Online sessions end. How you clutch this world, imagined --

IV. Epilogue: Or, Duga Considers the Future

Time passes. I imagine what my metal will become
once I'm dismantled, my parts recycled into something less
useless than I've been. I wonder if they'll need another frame
for her, if I can hold what's left of her particles --

But not often. Mostly, I think about how I'd be content as a
    shovel's blade,
breaking the earth. How the grandmothers would tamp
persistent feet against my step. How I'd be if my wires tamed
their gardens, small fence I'd make, inviting vines, inviting hope --

Time passes. I consider the needle in your small arm
a sort of beginning. Haven't I recycled this form
enough to know I can't keep out the world? I've tried --

After your first dose, we wander White Rock Lake, almost
alone, gray water beneath gray clouds. Like trust,
the wind knocks us a little. You hold my hand, then signal-like,
    break,

then fly --

Coda: Or, Chernobyl 2022

Khmelnitski, Rivne, South Ukraine.
Zaporizhzhia[4]; Russian-bombed maternity
hospitals, schools. Did I consider theories
I'd used, invented when I made the mistaken

assumption we'd all go unmasked?
Breathing became conspiracy. whispering
nostalgia. My children dancing
sanctuary away from sanctuary we'd claimed --

Chernobyl, I used you. Like my home,
I raked meaning around years. Melted down,
you were a ghost riding a train away from the cold

war that ended before my childhood. Returned
women, I used you. Shelter[5], disconnected from the grid,
hold, hold. A poem is never the way things end --

Footnotes

1. The High-frequency Active Auroral Research Program studies the ionosphere by heating it with high-frequency radio waves. Originally a project funded by the US military, HAARP is now maintained by the University of Alaska Fairbanks. HAARP has been the subject of many conspiracy theories, including those that accuse HAARP's researchers of controlling the weather for malicious purposes. The FAQ from which the title and quote have been taken can be found here: https://haarp.gi.alaska.edu/faq

2. *The Twa Sisters* is a British folk song that tells the story of jealousy between two sisters. The eldest's fiance loves the youngest sister better, so the eldest pushes her into the river. A miller finds her body and makes, alternately, a harp or a fiddle. The miller brings the instrument to court and plays for the sisters' family. The harp/fiddle sings reveals the eldest sister's crime. Many versions of this folk song exist. Like rumor, the main story tends to be the same across versions, but the details shift as the song progresses across time and place.

3. See SNOWIE (http://cswr.org/projects/snowie/) for an example of cloud seeding.

4. Nuclear Power Plants operational in Ukraine as of February 2022.

5. In March 2022, Russian forces disconnected the cooling shelter that prevented nuclear material at Chernobyl's Reactor 4 from the power grid from melting down the shelter and thus leaking.

Note for: "Fierce fighting in substantial numbers: ships damaged," In this story from the BBC World Service, news of the British invasion of the Falkland Islands begins with, as is customary, an announcement of the fighting and loss of ships and other large equipment. Only after this cataloging does the story move to the loss of human lives, both potential and actual.

While this does place the loss of ships and helicopters--literally-- before the human cost of the invasion, I reread this news story as working in the way that a sonnet can, even if that wasn't the BBC's original intent. One form of the sonnet builds an argument in its first eight lines, then a shift occurs in the argument in the remaining six. The initial argument can be reversed in the volta, or the turn, in the latter section of the poem.

Thus, I distilled the language of the news story into a sonnet. The loss of equipment sets up the tragedy of the lost lives, the heavier cost of war. I wanted to turn the idea of privileging metal over men-- as the news story seems to do--into one that concludes something quite different.

For the recording of my text, I left in artefacts of breath and pauses to mirror those of the news reader in the broadcast. I also distorted my voice and laid the static and pops of the received transmission over the poem, as I wanted my voice to be both of the language of the news story and of its reception over shortwave radio.

Acknowledgments

"Fierce fighting in substantial numbers: ships damaged," *Cities and Memory: Shortwave Transmissions Project*, January 2022

"1. Are There Any Long-term Effects of Ionospheric Heating?" and "8. Can HAARP Be Used To Generate VLF or ELF, that is Very Low Frequency or Extremely Low Frequency Signals?" *Jet Fuel Review*, Spring 2022 / Issue #23

"Transcript" and "When you asked, I was a diagram," *Eccentric Orbits: An Anthology of Science Fiction Poetry (vol. 3)*, April 2022

"CONELRAD 1960 / COVID 2020," *Fireside*, June 2022

"Chernobyl 1986 / COVID 2021," *Penumbric*, 2023

About the Author

T.D. Walker is the author of the poetry collections *Small Waiting Objects* (CW Books, 2019), *Maps of a Hollowed World* (Another New Calligraphy, 2020), and *Doubt & Circuitry* (Southern Arizona Press, 2023). Her poems and stories have appeared in *Strange Horizons, Fireside, Jet Fuel Review, The Cascadia Subduction Zone, Luna Station Quarterly,* and elsewhere. Walker curates and hosts *Line Break*, a program created for broadcast on shortwave radio that features poets reading their work. Find out more at https://www.tdwalker.net

Previous Works

Small Waiting Objects

Maps of a Hollowed World

www.ingramcontent.com/pod-product-compliance
Lightning Source LLC
Chambersburg PA
CBHW071849020426
42331CB00007B/1932